Hot Gourds

The Art of Pyrocarving

Beth Coheley

Mossy Oak Publishing LLC
Savannah

Published by Mossy Oak Publishing LLC
5710 Ogeechee Rd. Suite 200 #278, Savannah, GA 31405
(912) 414-8360
www.mossyoakpublishing.com

Coheley, Beth
Hot Gourds / Beth Coheley

ISBN-13:978-0-9845929-3-7
ISBN-13:978-0-9845929-6-8 (ebook)

Printed and bound in the United States of America

10 9 8 7 6 5 4 3 2 1

Contents

                    Hot Gourds

Introduction

I discovered the art of gourd making by complete accident. One Halloween I decided to make a Jack-O-lantern for my granddaughter, something she could pull out each year for the holiday. As an avid gardener, I knew that a gourd wouldn't rot if properly cleaned and prepared. I bought some cutting tools, made an orange pumpkin face, and ended up with a lifetime addiction to the joy and whimsy of gourd art.

Christmas decorations, geese with outstretched necks, shakers for the local high school sports fans, these were just a few of the possibilities I discovered, since gourds come in all shapes and sizes. The only limitation for a gourd artist is their imagination.

This book provides advanced instructions on the techniques of pyrocarving. I hope you enjoy creating your works of art as much as I do and find yourself a new hobby or another facet of one you may already have.

Enjoy!

Beth Coheley

Hot Gourds

Pyrocarving

Pyrocarving is a method used most often in wood working and design but can also be employed in the crafting of gourd art. Pyrocarving will allow more delicate cutting of gourds than standard metal tools. Less pressure is needed when using pyrography tools for carving, since the heat will do most of the work.

The wood burning tools allow an artist to carve or decorate gourds on an entirely different level.

Tools and Helpful Items

Cub-sized wood burner:

These may be purchased from any wood working supply company. Wood burning tips come in a variety of shapes and size, and you might want to choose a favorite company so all the tips will fit the wood burner. A quality wood burner will have adjustable heat settings and multiple tips.

For basic carving, you will need a tip that is approximately ¼ inch. This allows for fine carving as well as stability.

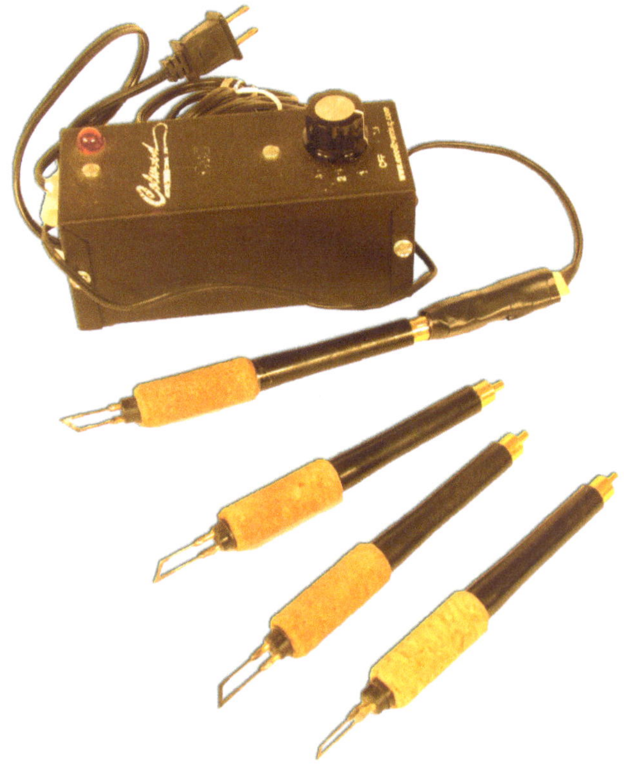

Hot Gourds

Pyrography paper:

This paper can be found online if you are not able to locate it at your local craft store. It is best for small designs or portions of a larger design.

Tracing paper:
Found at any craft store or online. This will allow you to transfer a chosen design to the gourd if you are not comfortable free-handing the lines you want to pyrocarve.

Stylus:
A wood, plastic, or metal stylus is perfect for tracing designs, but a ballpoint pen serves just as well!

Designs:
These can be found anywhere from wallpaper to your own imagination. Be creative!

Gloves:
If you feel the need for extra precaution, you can wear a pair of your choosing.

 Hot Gourds

Tips

Use scrap pieces of gourds to experiment with colors and wood burning tips before trying them on your work of art.

A wood burner with adjustable heat is important since the thickness of gourds varies. High heat on a thin gourd may cause unwanted damage, but low heat on a thick gourd will not cut sufficiently.

For coloring gourds, you can use craft paints, dyes, leather and shoe stains and even permanent markers. All work well for a variety of tones. The choice is yours.

Use gloves when working with stains to avoid staining hands.

If painting or staining the inside of a gourd, do so before carving to prevent spillage onto your design on the outside of the gourd

If using tracing paper, be sure it's facing toward the gourd. (You'd be surprised how easy it is to forget!)

Any stray marks from the tracing paper can be removed with a pencil eraser. Use a colored pen or pencil to trace with instead of a stylus to help ensure you have traced every line of your design.

Hot Gourds

Getting Started

You may start with a gourd for inspiration and find a design that is appropriate or you may choose a design then find a gourd that it will fit. Size and shape of your gourd can determine how best to use it.

Once you've picked your gourd and design, the next step is deciding how you plan to transfer the design onto the gourd. You have three options: Tracing paper, pyrography paper, and of course, you can always free hand it.

Tracing Paper

Simply cut your tracing paper to fit your design and tape it to the back side of the chosen design. Make sure the lighter side of the tracing paper is facing the design, leaving the brighter colored side exposed to place against the gourd.

Once you are satisfied that the two pieces of paper are flush, with no wrinkles, you can then tape them both to the gourd with the colored portion of the tracing paper facing the gourd.

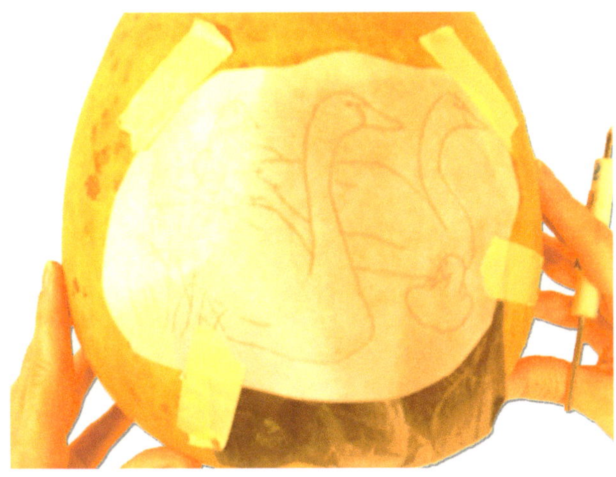

Once the paper is secured, trace the lines of your chosen design with a stylus or a colored pen or pencil. Using a pen or pencil will help you make sure all lines have been traced.

Remember, you can connect lines with your free hand if you've missed a small portion, and any mistakes or stray marks can be easily erased with a pencil eraser.

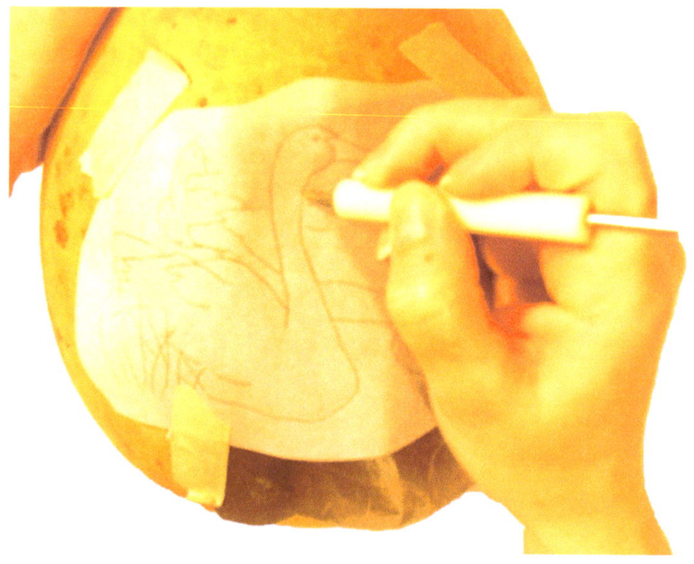

Purple and blue seem to be the best colors for tracing on gourds. Yellows or orange tones are too easily lost against the natural color.

Pyrography Paper

Pyrography paper is best suited for very simple designs. Complicated or very detailed patterns are less suited for pyrography paper due to the increased chance of error. Plus, you must trace or draw your pattern onto the pyrography paper itself before taping it to the gourd, and this adds another step.

Remember! If you use pyrography paper, you can't actually see what or where you are burning on the gourd until the paper is removed.

Below you can see an example of burning specific points of your design onto the gourd. If you burn these points when the paper is flush against the gourd, you will then have guide marks for replacing the pattern if you need to remove it to check your progress.

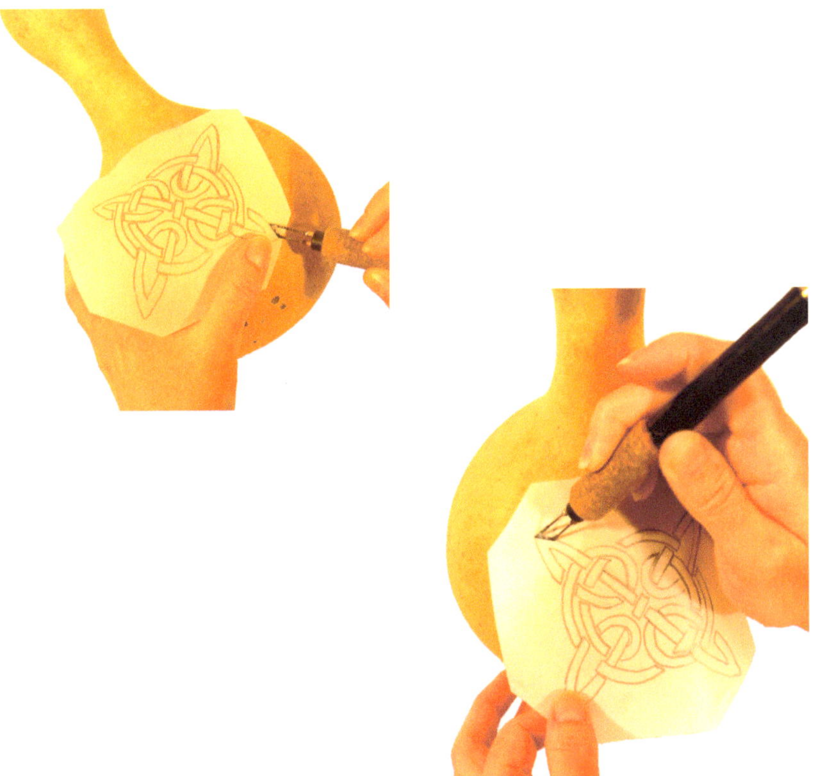

Free Hand

If you have a talent for drawing, you always have the option to free hand your pattern onto the gourd. If the design has no specific layout, or you want to use your creativity, this is also an option.

Hot Gourds

Shapes and Cut-outs

You can also create your own cut-outs or use household items to trace patterns onto gourds.

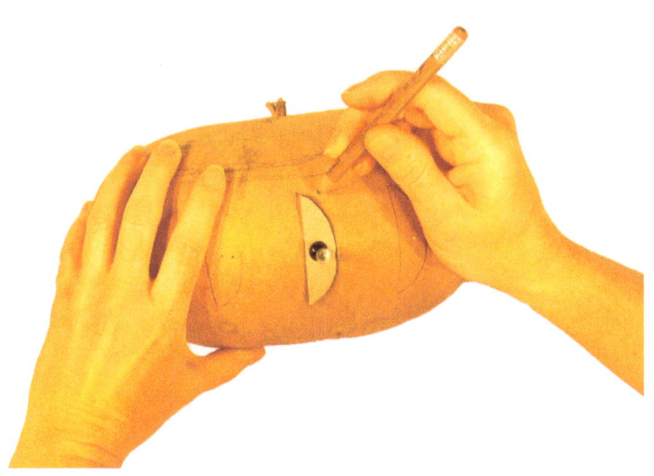

Regardless of your method, once your pattern is on the gourd you're ready to burn!

    Hot Gourds

Carving Technique

For pyrocarving, you will need a pointed tip, approximately ¼ inch. You should position the burner as shown in the picture below and carve in the direction indicated.

Notice that the tip is facing down toward the gourd but is positioned so the heated portion of the tip slices all the way through to ensure a clean carve.

If you are outlining a design, use a fine wood burning tip.

Wood burning tips come in a variety of shapes and sizes.

You can use the different sizes and shapes to score areas or create an endless array of designs.

                    Hot Gourds

Beth Coheley

Hot Gourds

Applying Color

If you simply plan to stain a carved gourd, apply chosen color while wearing gloves. Remember to apply color before carving if you don't want your paint or stain to bleed onto the inside of the gourd. The skin inside is very porous and will hold the color permanently.

Again, feel free to experiment. Some deep and beautiful colors come from permanent markers.

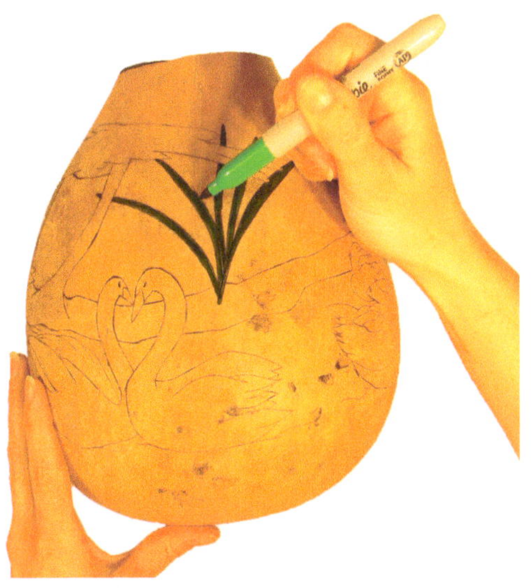

If you are applying color to a complicated pattern, you may also choose to do this before carving to help identify portions for cutting versus those you need to leave intact. You may also choose to paint one pattern before adding another if it helps give perspective. This is a personal choice.

Paint patterns completely. This will help you choose which portions need to be eliminated. Before you start cutting, you should ensure that each part of the design is connected to the base of the gourd that will remain intact or another piece of the pattern that is connected to the base, so you do not inadvertently cut away a portion of the design.

You may also want to ensure there are not any pieces that are too thin as they will be extremely fragile once the surrounding gourd is cut away.

Hot Gourds

From Start to Finish

Now let's go through the full process step by step.

Choose your gourd and your pattern then affix pattern to gourd using pyrography or tracing paper. For this example, we'll use tracing paper. Once applied and taped securely, trace your pattern with a stylus or pen.

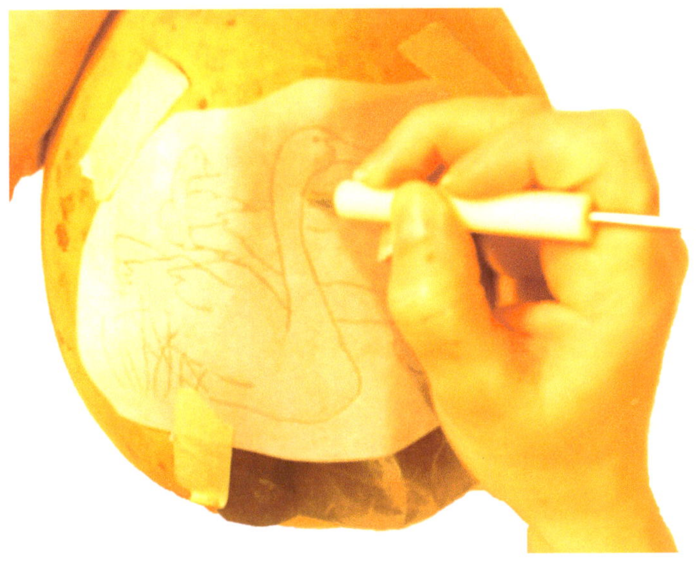

Once the pattern is applied, trace the lines with a fine wood burning tip, either a point or a thin blade as shown below. (If you so choose, you may go over your traced lines with a pencil for a darker outline before burning.)

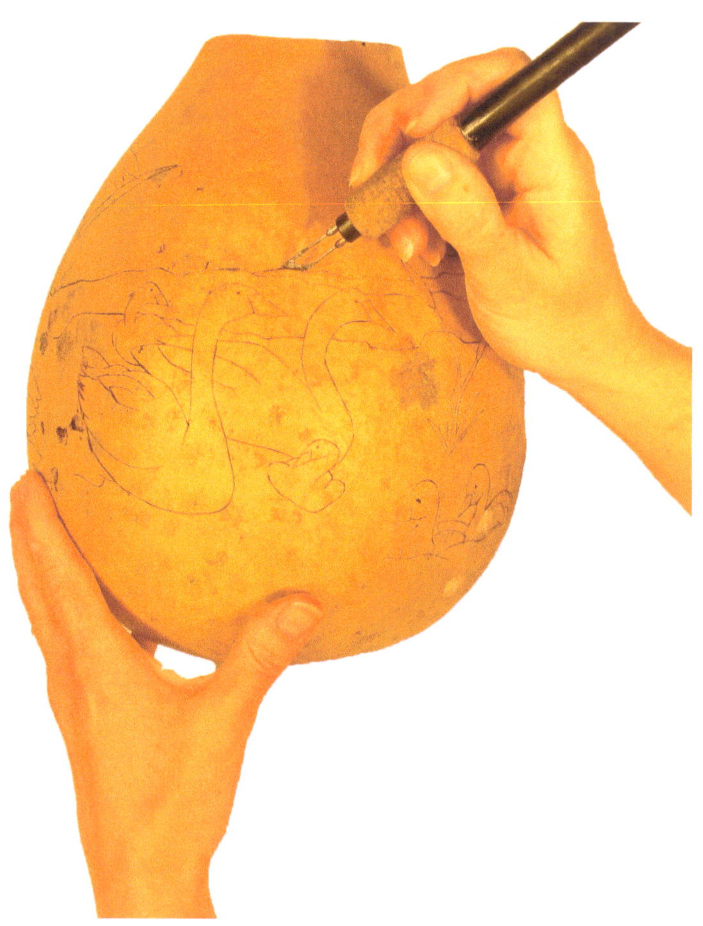

                    Hot Gourds

Before painting a gourd, you can use a wood filler or wood repair paste
to fill in any holes for a smoother finish.

Now you are ready to apply color, and you should do so before carving. The same applies for color or staining of the inside of the gourd! It is much easier to apply color to the inside of a full gourd than one already carved.

28

After you've colored your pattern, you can begin pyrocarving to remove unwanted portions. *Use caution!* Be sure you are not planning to carve away pieces that provide support or attachment for your design. It is heartbreaking to inadvertently remove a part of the design you have worked so hard on.

The process of carving will reveal the natural gourd once again. To cover this, you can use a flat wood burning tip to blacken the revealed edges or apply more paint or marker as an outline for your picture.

                    Hot Gourds

Continue carving and applying color as needed until you are satisfied with your results!

                    Hot Gourds

Beth Coheley

          Hot Gourds

www.ingramcontent.com/pod-product-compliance
Lightning Source LLC
Chambersburg PA
CBHW041227050726